WE BRAND YOU

HOW TO BUILD YOUR CLOTHING BRAND FROM SCRATCH TO 6-FIGURES

Creating. Results

CONTENTS

TESTIMONIALS

"Woo-hoo! Last month we hit our milestone from your course! I learnt so many gold nuggets here. Thank you warren, keep crushing it" - Steve Tan

"Thank you for the book. Going to be implementing the 3 pillars and the asap system every step of the way. Your marketing tips are gold too. Thank you" - Clothing by Angelo

"Such a great read and insightly addictive" - Xperian Gold

INTRO

Hi, I'm Warren from We Brand You. And this book is *How to Build Your Clothing Brand from Scratch to Six Figures.* At We Brand You, we're all about creating results.

Creating products that get you the results larger and faster.

I started composing and writing music around 13 years old. I've worked with a ton of uk and US artists including 50 cent, marques houston, so solid crew, skepta and wretch 32 to name a few.

It wasn't until around age 20 that I decided to take a break.

I was burnt out with not much money in a bank from managing my money poorly. I was also expecting my first son, so I decided to get a job in retail and selling property and jumped into marketing. And I had done those things for about five years.

It was around the age of 25 that I found a gap in the market and combined everything I learned from retail, from selling properties and in marketing, to applying it to We Brand You. So me and my older brother Clint, we've started We Brand You, and within about six months I was able to quit my full-time job. And just this year, it's February, which we're now in 2021, I've celebrated my 14,000th customer which is something I'm super, super proud of.

So the lesson and a major takeaway from my story so far that I will say to anyone and I share it all the time, is take breaks and don't quit.

When I was 20, things felt like they couldn't get any worse. I felt like I was taking a backward step, I felt the pressure to put food on my table for my family. But I didn't quit, I found myself, got back in the game at age 25.

Like I said, celebrating my 14,000th customer this year. So

that's something I want to show you how you can do the same,

take control of your situation and really multiply your results.

CHAPTER 1

THE HUSTLE

S/o who is We Brand You? Our mission, our vision is to be the world's number one online academy for clothing brand startups. To engage, to grow and expand your products and services internationally. I quickly found there are not many companies or brands that are dedicated to clothing brands. To help them create a clothing brand from scratch to six figures. How was it done? So these are some of our wins. These are some of the cool things that we've been able to do.

We've worked with Link Up TV, Mixtape Madness, Geordie Shore, MTV, loads of different celebrities and loads of different artists, too many to write here.

We also worked with Wembley Arena to do merchandise for their concerts and their tours and stuff. And we worked with loads of different clothing brand startups, over a thousand different upcoming clothing brand startups.

Now, here's where I found the biggest problem. I found that out of all of the people we worked with, 80% of clothing brand startups would not come back to place a repeat order. I'll say that again. 80% of the clothing brands that we worked with wouldn't come back a second time and place a repeat order.

Why is this? Most clothing brands don't know what they're doing. I don't know if this is you or someone you know but you get an idea, you start making t-shirts, you try and sell it to your family and friends, you start an Instagram page and then it dies out. You don't get any sales, you're left with all of the stock in your house, in your bedroom, taking up space, you've lost money, you feel embarrassed, you don't know what to do, you've told everyone your dreams of what you want to do with your brand but you've failed, so you don't go back to place another order because you've quit.

Having a low customer return rate sucked for us because we weren't constantly making profit from our customer base; and it sucked for our customers because they were failing, they were wasting money. So then we would be on the phone to them, asking them if they would like to place another order but they'd reply "No thanks, I've still got to stock from my first order".

So after hearing that time and time again, we started to feel their pain and we knew where we needed to shift our focus and where we could be of service the most. We realised we were better off shifting our focus from just being a printing and embroidery company (which there's so many of them out there anyway.

If you go to your local high Street, you'll see hundreds of them) to actually being a coaching and online academy dedicated to coaching and educating inexperienced clothing brands on how to build a clothing brand from scratch to six figures

This book is designed to provide the solution to no longer having wasted inventory, wasting your money and pissing it down the drain. No more begging friends and family to buy from you, no more feeling like a failure and no more wasting time. Life is too precious to be wasting it on things that you know nothing about, and things that you're destined to fail from. All you need is a coach, like the great phrase legendary speaker and author Jim Rohn once said *success leaves clues.*

CHAPTER 2
YOU HAVE NO IKEA

M y philosophy can be compared to the IKEA concept.

Imagine you go to IKEA. You're shopping with your partner, your friend, or whoever it is and you're trying to find some wardrobes for your bedroom. You buy it, you go to the checkout, you purchase it, you take it home and now you guys take it out of the box and you start trying to put it together. But what you find is, there's no manual inside the box. Are you going to be able to put that wardrobe together successfully?

Now the chances are, you might be able to. But for me, when I bought a desk from IKEA in the past, there was a time where I didn't have the manual. I actually ended up putting the backboard on the wrong way. It got to a point where I just thought, you know what, let me just leave it, it looks okay anyway. But what most people are doing, they're trying to put their clothing brand together without an instruction manual, without knowing exactly what to do.

So they end up doing it wrong, and just leaving it, forgetting about it or trying to create a brand and sell it, and it doesn't feel right. So customers are coming along to your brand and it's not getting the right feeling because you've set it up wrong. So instead of trying to assemble the wardrobes by yourself, or trying to put together this clothing brand by yourself, you actually need a manual.

You could put it together yourself, but it's going to take a lot more time, you're going to waste a lot of energy, and you're going to be confused half the time. Now something that would normally take about half an hour is probably now going to take three or four hours. And even when it's complete, like when I put my desk together, it might be wobbly, unstable, or it might even be dangerous. You must use an instruction manual. However, there is no instruction manual in today's market for new clothing brands.

So when we shifted our focus, we looked at what was out there that could actually coach you and give you a step-by-step walkthrough on how to create a six figure brand from scratch.

On the path to success, there's so many different clothing brand startups trying to grow in today's market, and you're one of them. You're actually probably doing it the long and hard way. So like I said, we've designed this manual to give you clear instructions and direction to basically just assemble your own clothing brand from scratch to six figures with no more guesswork, no more confusion, no more time wasting. There is a blueprint to follow, and this is that.

Now we just want to put out there that we can't guarantee results. We can guarantee that our systems work **only** if you work.

You have to commit to it, you have to follow it through hard work, discipline, being teachable and being willing to learn and dedicating yourself to not just learning this manual, but going through it over and over again and applying what you learn.

If information was enough we'd all be rich, skinny and healthy but sadly it isn't. Action is the bridge between information and results

Don't just learn it; put it into action as well.

CHAPTER 3

TRAFFIC JAM

There is a good saying I like that we created here at We Brand You, and it's

why you get stuck in traffic towards your goal, when you can drive down the fast lane to success?

And we like to think of this book, this information, and this system as the fast lane to success which we've worked with so many other brands in the past and we've sat down, we've consulted with them, and we've managed to get them huge results based on this system that we're now sharing with you. And if you follow the same system as well and you dedicate yourself to it, there's no reason why you can't drive down the fast lane to success too.

So let's talk a little bit about the market. So I don't know if you know, but the clothing industry is a 4.6 billion pounds industry worldwide and you have to be aware of the potential.

There will always be a need for clothing in this world. There isn't always going to be a need for technology, because technology comes and goes. There were tape cassettes, then we went to CDs, then we went to DVDs and now most people listen to music on digital download or streaming.

Same with cars; cars are constantly evolving. The three things that don't usually evolve are houses, food and shelter. Now they may change slightly in design etc, but there's always going to be a huge demand for clothing, food and shelter.

Clothing is one of the big three. So you need to be positioning your clothing line in a way that speaks directly to your ideal buyer.

So let's summarise:

we know there is a market, we know it's a profitable market and it's growing year on year and we know it's one of the big three

Now you need to decide how you're going to position yourself in a way that's going to speak to a specific person to get them to become a buyer. But we'll discuss that and talk about that more a bit later.

Another word of inspiration that I love says this,

Treat your brand like a business and it will pay you like a business; treat it like a hobby and it will pay you like a hobby.

And guess what? Hobbies don't pay very well.

You need to treat your clothing brand like a business. Set it up with a good foundation so that it can pay you like a business. Way too many startups make the mistake of getting started and only giving it a try. It's something that they're just trying, it's a hobby, they're just "seeing" if it works. Don't just "see" if it works, because chances are it won't.

Commit to it, treat it like a business and it will pay you like a business.

CHAPTER 4

3 PILLAR TARGETING

W e're going to dive into targeting and speaking about how to attract your ideal buyer.

I was speaking to a client last week, and asked him 'who is your target audience?'

And like 805 of newbies replied 'everyone can kind of wear my stuff, my stuff is for everyone.'

This is a deadly mistake I want you to avoid. They want to target everyone because they think it will mean more sales but it actually does the opposite. Because in life by trying to please everyone, we end up pleasing no one. See, it's not about coming in and having a product that can fit everyone or suit everyone, it's not about that. It's about niching down, picking a specific set of people and just catering to that specific set. It's not about trying to cater to everyone, because like I said, by trying to please everyone, you'll end up pleasing no one.

So we like to say there are three pillars of effective targeting. It starts with a:

- message

- story

- audience

So what do I mean by this? A message is, for example, **an apple a day keeps the doctors away.**

That's a message, like a philosophy or a saying.

And then you want to connect a story with your message.

For example,

I've been working 9-5, my health had really deteriorated. I was working double shifts, and I got burnt out. I went to the doctor and my doctor said I had low health. And my doctor joked and said, "you know what, you need to actually start with an apple a day and start looking after yourself and taking care of your health." So I then decided to create a clothing brand as a symbol of inspiration for myself and others to take care of their health whilst grinding before it's too late

This is an example of an effective story that compliments the message superbly

The beauty of this process is that once you have your story nailed, the audience jumps right out off the page. The target audience in this case would be 'people who have 2 jobs or work double shifts that eat poorly and neglect their health to make money instead'

So now you've got your message, your story and your audience. Your message is an apple a day keeps the doctors away.

Your story is, your double shift, you got burnt out, the doctor said, start with an apple a day, and you've got your audience. People that are like you, fellow nine-to-fivers burning out their health, that need to stop, take care.

Now you might think, 'yeah, but this sounds nothing like a clothing brand. I just want to make quality clothing.'

You can make quality clothing, but people don't just buy clothes for the sake of it, they buy clothes because of the message embedded deep inside the brand.

People don't just buy Nike because it's Nike. Nike is just a tick. It's nothing, it's the message behind it, Just Do It.

Nike inspires action, they inspire you, they motivate you, to move to take action, to do something with yourself. That's what you're actually buying into on a deep subconscious level

Most people don't realise this. It's the brand, like Apple; that

Apple ogi that people buy all around the world, they inspire technology and advancement. So you're not just buying a laptop, you're buying that cool, trendy thing. When you go to a coffee shop, and you see someone sitting on their laptop with an apple logo on it, they're inspiring the future, they're moving forward, it's the feeling of belonging to the small crowd of coolness.

So it's all about understanding the psychological aspect of why people buy.

Another message, story and audience example is my own story

Message:

take breaks and don't quit.

Story:

Age 13, I wanted to impact the world through music. Age 20, I had to quit my dreams and get a real job because I was having a son, and at age 25 I returned, applied everything I had learned in my marketing and sales jobs to go on to launch my 4 online companies and impact thousands and thousands of people worldwide.

Audience:

Men aged 25 - 44 chasing their dreams, wanting to make something of themselves, but getting battered by reality. wanting to do something with themself. Wanting to challenge the status quo and provide for their family,

When you have your message, story and audience, you don't even have to think about what logo it is going to be now, or your designs. You already get a feeling and an idea for where your art work is going to go. As opposed to trying to figure out what the artwork should be first?

When you know your message, your story and your audience? The logo and artwork will naturally come to you based on the picture your story paints.

Here's a few other popular stories with clever message and stories buries inside them

Toy Story - The message inside Toy Story is that **friends are for life.** The story of Woody and Buzz clearly demonstrates this.

A Bug's Life - the message in that story is **heroes are not about size.** They're bugs, they're small, they go on a journey, and they're trying to defeat the grasshoppers.

Monsters Inc. - the message is **things are not really what they seem right.** They're monsters, but being scary is only their job.

And last but not least is Finding Nemo. The message is that **no ocean is too large to cross for the ones you love.**

These are all massive films that we know and love. We know and love these characters, but It's the message that we carry after we've watched a film that stays with us.

So that is the message in these stories and this is what I'm trying to drill into your head whilst you're starting your clothing brand start-up, to understand your message, have a good compelling story and target a specific set of people that are going to resonate with your message, resonate with your story, so that you can sell to them.

It's really important that -- If you take anything away from this book take away this. Understand your story, your message and your audience and I'll guarantee you, I promise you, it will make everything else fall into place and make it so much easier for you. I promise.

CHAPTER 5

THE A.S.A.P SYSTEM

I coined this system myself, the ASAP system. The ASAP system stands for:

Artwork, Supplier, Acquire and Produce.

Now like I said, once you've set up your message, your story and your target audience, you're going to want to go into the ASAP system. And the first step in the ASAP system is artwork.

You're going to base your artwork on the three pillar targeting system because you now have the foundation, the direction and the theme for your artwork.

S is for suppliers. You want to hire a reliable supplier that will save you a ton of time, a ton of money and a ton of energy.

The A stands for acquire, which means you always want to acquire a sample before buying. This is crucial. We've made tons of mistakes in the past, lost thousands and thousands of pounds from not following this rule. So you definitely want to get samples beforehand, before buying. Sounds simple, but you'd be surprised how many people get stung here.

And the P is for produce. You want to mass produce and then prepare for a launch.

So let's go ahead and break down the ASAP system a little bit further.

A is for the Artwork. There's two ways you can do artwork. You can either hire someone professional to do it for you, or you can do it for yourself for free. Now, I'm always going to advise you to pay a premium, because you're going to get quality back. So whatever you put into this clothing brand, is what you're going to get out. Like I said earlier, if you treat it like a hobby and you try and design things yourself, it's going to pay you like a hobby. If you treat it like a business and you invest in it, you hire high-quality artwork, designers, graphic designers, web developers, then you're going to get a return and it's going to pay you rewards in ways you I couldn't imagine.

So, premium ways you can use Fiverr, you can use Upwork, you can google graphic designers, or if you've got a friend that does artwork or graphic design, then you can take on a referral.

If you don't have the budget for it and you're trying to do it for free, then you can use sites like Canva, you can download Photoshop, you can use Easil, or you can use Visme. These are remarkable websites for designing artwork as well. So don't be afraid to use those if you're on a budget. But if you want my opinion, it's always best to go for a premium service, but both of these systems work.

S is for Suppliers. And a question that we always get asked is "should I find a supplier in my own country or overseas?"

Now, you're going to want to use both, ultimately. But I'm going to show you how to use both effectively. You want to use your own country first and then transfer everything overseas. The good thing about your own country is that there's good communication, because obviously, you both speak the native country language, so you can get things done quicker, emails are done quicker, you're not going to go back and forth and spend so much time understanding and translating what your supplier is saying.

There is quicker shipping time, so something that will take you three weeks coming from abroad will maybe take you 2-3 days to receive it.

So you'll be able to sell more products and have a larger range, and always restock much quicker. But the benefits of going overseas is you've got lower costs.

So you're buying bulk, and you'll be able to get it for under maybe $5-$10 depending on what it is.

So you're going to cut your costs which is going to mean more profit in the long run. You're going to have access overseas to larger custom fabric selections like silks, cashmere, and many other material combinations that you can think of.

Last but not least, they're going to have faster production times, simply because they've got factories, they've got staff, they're used to doing much higher run rates than smaller shops in your country because ultimately a lot of these overseas factories are located in manufacturing districts.

So homeland and overseas have pros and cons but I always

advise to find a local supplier when you're on the come up, and then transfer everything over to overseas.

For example, once you're selling 10,000 per month revenue, start looking at ways to get it overseas like Pakistan, India, China, so that you can start increasing your margins, having access to more different fabrics, and growing in that space. Slowly work yourself up and then once you're in the big leagues and you want to do more, you want to grow, you want to expand: find a good supplier overseas.

If you want access to the suppliers overseas, we have a quality product on our website called The Clothing Connect Manufacturers list. So this is a direct list of all of -- Let's be real. The manufacturing industry is full of sharks, it's brutal. I could tell you, me and my partner and my wife, like we can sit down and tell you stories of the amount of times we've been stung by manufacturers abroad.

They have all different ways of doing things, and a lot of them are just money hungry predators. They will run off with your money if you're not careful. And that's why we created The Clothing Connect just to help navigate the industry.

It's like a little black book of our main suppliers that we've worked with, I think 15 - 20 different manufacturers in there, Turkey, India, China, and reliable suppliers that you can reach out to, hit them up, emails, phone numbers, and message them and place orders confidently.

Now, I'll still say get samples because like I said, samples are crucial but it's giving you a better way of doing things and lessening the chance of you getting stung. So I felt like it was important for us to do that for you, just to help you navigate the shark infested manufacturers industry.

A is for Acquiring. This is where you acquire and

order your samples.

Note: you always want to request a sample first and foremost, like I said. Always move the conversation to WhatsApp for faster communication as soon as possible. Only order from reliable companies that have more than five years of trading. Now, if you can find a company that has traded more than 10 years, excellent! Even better. But a minimum of five years trading is important.

Don't want to order from someone that has just come into the game six months ago, and they're using you as a guinea pig or they're using you as a way to get their feet on the ground and find their way. You're nobody's test dummy.

Only ever work with people that know what they're doing as this will save you time and money

Last but not least, you want to ask to see photos of the sample before they ship because it's all good receiving a sample, but if you don't like the sample, you gotta send it back to them. And then they're going to have to send it back to you. So you could save a lot of time if you just request a picture sample, before they ship. For example if the zippers are out of place before they ship, the picture will show this and you can say ``I didn't want you to put the zipper there, I wanted you to put the zipper on the back or the side" and they'll make the changes.

Get as much information in the photo before they ship, it speeds up the process.

Alibaba.com is an online wholesale marketplace where you can buy products in bulk. It's a massive place where literally, they've got hundreds of thousands of different products. And one of the things they have is clothing.

You have the choice of buying a single item, if you negotiate with a supplier, and they agree to sell you one item, not all the time they do but you can get samples. However the real benefit of

Alibaba is the ability to work directly with a manufacturer.

20 years ago, you would have had to fly to these countries, gone to the manufacturing districts, have meetings with them and sit down with someone to build a relationship with them and place an order, but nowadays, thanks to the internet, you get to just speak to these manufacturers like it's nothing.

So it's made it 10 times easier and that's why for the first time ever we're seeing the most multimillionaires come up more than any other time in the world because of the internet.

Having access and direct access to these sorts of things just makes you more profitable and allows you to make more money in the marketplace

One of the things I would say in Alibaba though, is to always make sure you find a company that has trade insurance. Always pay within Alibaba so that you stay eligible for the trade insurance.

The trade insurance is simply to protect you if you buy a product and they send a wrong/damaged product.

You'll be able to open up a case and be covered to get your money back. So trade insurance is important.

Now, do I recommend that it be all and end all? No. But when you're getting started and a little bit unsure, it's always good to be covered by trade insurance. So one of the cool things with reaching out to suppliers is that we have an opening script message that works like a charm. Like I said, we're all about saving you time and saving you money. And this opening script has been perfectly crafted, we've used it for years now. It's perfectly crafted to just fast track the whole communication space of ordering products. So it starts off with:

Hello, my name is *insert your name here* and I'm searching for a reliable supplier of XYZ. I came across your company in my research and wanted to get some further *information regarding and then you put in your quantities and XYZ. So could you please get back to me as soon as possible with the above information? My email is XYZ, my WhatsApp is da da da da da. Thank you and I'm looking forward to hearing from you. Hopefully I can place an order with your company.*

Kind regards,

insert your first and last name here

P is for Produce. So once your sample arrives,

what's next? It's time to PRODUCE and this script below is the perfect script to order and take it from samples to producing your next order and getting the best deal. So here it is.

Dear *enter companies name*,

We've received and tested the samples you've sent. I'm happy to say that the quality of the products was up to the standard we need to be able to use you as a supplier. So now we are ready to place an order of high quantity, however, to meet our quality rules for purchasing from new suppliers, we would like to order 200 pieces rather than our usual amount of 500. That way we can test everything at a higher scale and also get feedback from our returning customers. Once this order is complete, and as long as everything goes well, we can then use your factory as a primary supplier for all future orders. So please get back to me as soon as possible so we can arrange the order details.

Kind regards, Your name.

Now this is going to allow you to move from sample phase to production phase. And with these things you want to get a supplier -- The supplier is always going to try and push you to place a bigger order. But most of the time they're going to settle for a lower order as well, but they will try and push you. I have seen it time and time again.

They will make you feel like they won't work with you unless you place a big order but trust me, you have to stand your ground, and know that they will accept a lower MOQ.

And that's what's so cool about the last script that I just said. It's key to almost making them prove themselves to you and for them to sell you on why YOU should be working with THEM.

Similar to the TV show, The Voice. The artist sings and then judges turn their seats if there interested and then they start selling themselves on why the contestant should choose them. Its at that point the contestant has all the power and control You want to be in a position of power all the time when you're negotiating therefore that script that I just showed you puts you as the person that's like:

"ok, tell me why I should work with you. Sell me on why I should choose your factory instead of the other 100 - 200 other factories out there? Why should I work with you?"

That's what negotiation is always about, and will always be

about. It's about who has the leverage? Who is in a position of power? The person in a position of power, who has the leverage can negotiate better terms, better conditions, and all of that stuff.

The fact that you've had some previous contact with the company because you've gotten samples, you've ordered them, your communication is good, *because you're using our script, wink wink,* they'll now view you as a serious buyer with what we call 'buyer's intent'. And that's the highest level of professionalism you can show to any business or company out there. If you're showing buyer's intent - you're a serious buyer. People will treat you with professionalism all the time, and it puts you in a good position. So just remember that.

So that is the 'ASAP system'. We had the three pillar targeting system and this was the 'ASAP system' which consists of artwork, supplier, acquire and produce.

Once you've finished the ASAP system, you're going into your six figure launch pad.

We've created a pre-launch checklist, which basically you just want to tick off to make sure that you're on track to get ready to launch in the best way possible, and profit in the best way possible as well.

CHAPTER 6

SIX FIGURE LAUNCH PAD

S tage one of the pre-launch is you want to choose your online store.

Shopify is highly recommended. I've worked with Wix, I've worked with Square, I've worked with Shopify, I've worked with WordPress as well. And hands down, Shopify is the best platform of all. I love their back end system, you can really see your stats, your traffic, it's just clearer and I love that *Ka-Ching* sound that goes off every single day. There is no better feeling. So I definitely recommend Shopify.com to build your online store

Stage two of the pre-launch is choosing a domain name that

matches your social media. So if your brand is called Chili Peppers on social media, you want to make sure that Chili Peppers is what it's called on your domain name because nothing's worse than people finding you on social media and then trying to type it into URL but can't find you because your names don't match. So you need to make a conscious decision to make sure that all of the social media and your URL names always match; just for maximum visibility and so that people can always find you. Otherwise you will lose sales hands down.

Stage three on a pre-launch is customizing your store OR hiring a web designer.

Now you can do the customization yourself. But again, I'm always going to advise you to hire someone professional. Here's the thing, when you hire a professional, you're going to get professional results. If you try and do it yourself, you're going to get mediocre to probably poor results, most of the time.

Now, sometimes you can strike lucky. But if you just don't know what you're doing, how can you guarantee that it's going to work? So always invest, invest, invest. And I like to see it as this. When someone wants to open up a bakery or when someone wants to open up a lawyer or an accounting firm, or a McDonald's franchise, they always go to the bank and they take money from the bank to invest in these projects. Since your clothing brand startup is a real business too, this shouldn't not be any different.

If you want to treat it like a serious business, you need to borrow money, go to the bank, or whatever it is, or use your savings and invest in your clothing business. Because guess what? Investments pay you a return. All too often I don't see people going to banks or lending money because they don't really believe it's going to work. And guess what? If you don't believe it's going to work, it's not gonna.

Getting an investment, finding the money and doing these

things, really prove to yourself more than anything and your subconscious that this is going to work. Otherwise, you wouldn't have borrowed the money.

So you want to set the foundation strong from the get-go.

Stage four in the pre-launch checklist is to add clothing inventory to your store.

You don't have to always start with 10-20 different pieces, start small, maybe:

  ➢ 1, 2, 3 different clothing pieces,
  ➢ good logos on them
  ➢ good designs
  ➢ add them to your store
  ➢ set the pricing right
  ➢ make sure you're competitive
  ➢ make sure you've sorted out your postage and packaging
  ➢ make sure you've got everything in place

so that when a customer comes to your store, they can buy.

You also want to take good pictures. You and your friends (or hire a model or an artist, your local photographer) can take some really good pictures for your website because a picture speaks a thousand words.

Don't be afraid to use your phone as most phones are HD nowadays.

So you're going to be able to get really good pictures from your phone. But again, don't be afraid to hire a professional either.

Stage five is to set up a payment processor and PayPal, add them to your website. It's really simple.

And stage six, last but not least, is to launch the store and make sales. That's your six figure launch.

Congratulations, you're ready to launch. You've got your website down, you've got your clothing, you've got the best prices because you've used our scripts, you've got your message, you've got your story, you've got your target audience, you've got everything set up, you've properly prepared yourself for success. But this is the part where most people fail.Simply because they just depend on their family and friends to buy their clothes, or to "support them".

Once you run out of friends and family to sell to, once you've finished posting in your social media to your friends and family, and no one supports you, you're going to get angry with them.

You're nan didn't buy your jumper so now you're pissed off at her, you stopped going around to your family's house on a Sunday because no one is supporting your vision, your dream. And this is where people get angry and they quit. They thought everyone would rush in and buy their clothes. But guess what, that ain't a sustainable business model,

Not by any stretch of the imagination, so there is no point. And this is where I said at the beginning, growing a clothing brand from scratch to six figures is a mindset thing.

It's all about getting rid of the poor mindset thinking and really putting better things in place, putting a mindset in place. And one of the things is not relying on your family or friends. If they support you *whoopie*, good, good on them, good for you. But don't rely on them because it's not a sustainable business model.

Like Paul Jang says *traffic is king*. Whoever controls the traffic is king. Especially online now more than ever, if you can get loads of traffic to your website then you're going to make sales. The average conversion rate online is about 2%, meaning out of 100 people that hit your website, out of every 100 on average you're going to get 2 sales.

Now I've seen websites that have a 5% conversion rate, which means out of every 100 they get 5 sales. But on average, you're looking at about 2%, whether you're Argos, JD Sports, Footlocker, eBay, Amazon, all of these websites average between 2% - 4%.

What a great world it would be if we had 80% conversion rates, meaning 80% of people bought? But it's not, that's just how it is.

It's the law of averages. It's just how it is. So if you can control your traffic, then you will just make sales. It's just a no brainer, it's just how it is. And it's actually called the 80/20 traffic rule.

So imagine owning a store, walk with me. Imagine you owned a store in an abandoned shopping complex, in a deserted town. Now your shop is open, but there are cobwebs growing in every corner of the store. You've wasted a ton of money on goods that you've never been able to sell. That's what it's like when your website has no traffic. Basically, you've got a store in an abandoned complex in a deserted town, and there are cobwebs growing all around your shop. That's what it's like having an online store and not driving any traffic to it. For me, as a marketer, any marketer will tell you we're obsessed with traffic. We're just obsessed with it. You need to get obsessed with driving people to your website.

But the good thing about it is now you can actually pay for traffic, so you can pay to get people to your website. So if you're spending $1 to drive someone to your website and they buy, then you're always going to be in profit. So if you spend 30 pounds, do this math, quick maths.

You spent 30 dollars to get 100 people to your website, and you're selling a T-shirt for 25 dollars each. And like I said, out of every 100 people, you're going to get roughly about three sales. So if three people purchase one t-shirt, at 25 dollars each, that is 75 dollars you've made from those three customers. And like I said, you've paid 25 pounds for those 100 customers. So you've made 50 dollars profit, you've spent 25 dollars, you've made 75 dollars.

So 25 minus 75 is 50 dollars, you've made profit. So that's how you have to see it. It's a simple formula that you pay for your traffic.

You don't want to bother your friends, you don't bother your family, because they've got kids to raise, they've got work to do, they've got food to cook, they have got families that they -- don't waste time on them, running them down. Simply go out and pay for traffic, invest in a traffic system, a traffic source to your website and make money. And this, we've done constant coaching calls on this website alone, because traffic is key, traffic is king.

So this slide is how to send insane amounts of traffic to your website, and bank massive profit. Now one of the things you could do is run paid ads on social media. So that's your Instagram, that's your Facebook, that's your Twitter, that's your YouTube. Set up a five dollars a day budget on all of these platforms and whichever one brings you sales, you focus the majority of your time onto that channel.

So if you set up Instagram, Facebook, Twitter, YouTube, and guess what, your Twitter pops off, and it gives you the most sales because you'll be able to track all these things. If it gives you the most sales, then 80% of your marketing budget now goes into Twitter and just leave the rest of the 20% in the other channels and just let it run, because you're going to be in a profit zone.

The second one works the same, except it's for Google ads instead. So you set up Google Ads, set up that when people are searching on Google, I don't know. Say they're searching for exercise equipment. If you're a gym brand and you've got a gym clothing brand, now your product can show up.

Your t-shirt can show up in the search result. So if someone is searching for exercise equipment, the chances are they may be interested in exercise gear as well. So they might click your ad, come to your website, like the look of the t-shirt or like the look of the sports bra or whatever it is you've got there, and they might purchase it. They might just leave and not care and go what the hell was that?

But guess what they might actually stay and buy it if it's good enough, and it convinces them to buy and it's a good price or whatever. So you want to pay for ads on Google ads as well.

The third one is you want to pay for fashion influencers to repost. We've all seen it and whether it's 'The only way is essex' or the celebrities and the singers, music artists? you can pay these people to wear your clothing. Now it's always going to be more effective than paid ads because when you're running ads on social media, you're showing your product to people that have never come into contact with your brand before.

So there's going to be an element of distrust there, they're going to really see and trust that your products are good because they've never tried it before, they don't know anyone that's tried it. But if you use a fashion influencer, then that fashion influencer has access to thousands and thousands of people and their audience, and their audience trusts them.

That's why their audience is following them because they trust them. So if you send out a t-shirt to the influencer, they're going to want to promote it to their brand, it's simple. It's simple. We all know what a fashion influencer is and if you don't check it out online. Sometimes an influencer will just ask for the product. You send it to them and they will post it or sometimes they want money. It just depends.

You gotta work it out, you got to negotiate and you got to come to a price that is going to be good for you. Remember to stay in the profit zone. Always try to remember to stay in the profit zone and negotiate, so you get the best price.

The fourth one is to post video content on YouTube, this is another good one. So if you got workout gear, you want to post or work with maybe a personal trainer, shoot videos, some

exercises, upload it to YouTube, they're going to be wearing your gear, you can drop a link in the description box below so that people watching the video can go back to your website and click the link and buy the gear that they can see.

You want to create content around your brand, like I said, if we use an example of an apple a day to keep the doctor away analogy of the message earlier, you could post different nutritional tips, to help people not burn out. To help people stay fit whilst they're on the hustle, so they're not just neglecting their health.

Create content around these things but you subtly drop your clothing brand in those videos. You subtly drop the link in the description box below. This is called content marketing, you're marketing your product through providing high value content. It works like a charm. I've got a music blog, as well as We Brand You. Like I said, I've got a music blog because music is one of my passions. I've got a music blog online, called Thir13een.com.

I drop loads of different content about different music reviews and things like that. And I have a link in the description box below, which drives them back to my website, where we sell products that help them sound better and become more. It's simple, it's a simple process.

They like the content, so they want to get more and buy premium products that can continue to help them sound better and become more. It's a win-win for everyone.

Fifth on the list is capturing emails and sending out discount codes twice a month. So the first time you send out an email is at the beginning of the month when everyone gets paid. And you send out the second one in the middle of the month where people usually get paid if they get paid weekly, or bi-weekly.

Next is to run competitions and giveaways. So give away a few t-shirts, get people to promote your brand. So it's basically saying if you want to win a free t-shirt or a free tracksuit bottom, repost this image and tag two friends. What you're going to find is you're going to get loads of people reposting your stuff and tagging their friends.

So you're increasing your awareness. Those friends are seeing it and also reposting and then you'll get this kind of network of people that are reposting and tagging, reposting and tagging, and that is doing a lot of the promotion of your brand for you. Most of the time when people enter a competition, if they lose, they'll still go ahead and buy your product anyway, because they already showed an interest to you, and also to themselves and they know they're interested. So they'll be like, well, I didn't win the competition but I still want the products, so I'll go and buy anyway, it works. It works hands down.

So it's a real, real effective way of marketing your products.

Second to least is to collaborate with other brands in your industry. So if you're in fitness, you can work with other fitness brands. If you're into urban wear you can work with urban artists and music artists. If you're into health, you can work with health nutritionists; whatever your target market is, find out what other things they like that you can link up with and then everyone, both brands can benefit from both audiences.

And last but not least, is to blog the latest news in your industry. You can use the video content that you post to YouTube, you can also post that to your blog, which is going to show up in Google and Google will start indexing you and adding you to the Google search engines. And it's another way to build community, build content and drive sales. So to send insane amounts of traffic to your website, these are my Bibles.

CHAPTER 7

CLOSING

I don't stray away from these things at all. If you want to build a clothing brand from scratch to six figures, this is how you do it. Stop relying on your friends and family. Do not do it! Don't embarrass yourself, you just don't need to do it. Because even if you got everyone to buy your product anyway, who are you going to use after that. They can't get you to six figures, they won't be able to get you six figures alone.

You're going to need to reach out to other people and this is where a lot of people fail because they just don't know how or they try and they fail.

So if you're someone that's tried these things in the past, go back and try it again. Go back, try it again. Keep going back and doing it over and over again till guess what? One day it's going to work one day, it's just going to work and it's going to click for you and you're going to understand why it wasn't working before and why it's suddenly working now. That's the difference.

The trouble is if you've tried these things before and you haven't built a sale it's because you didn't know what you were doing and you're trial and error. And in life there's a time for sowing and there's a time for reaping. Running these ads and doing these things is you sowing your seed. You cannot expect to sow and reap in the same season.

When you plant a seed in spring, your sweet corn does not grow until the end of summer. You do not plant a sweet corn seed in the patch and then two weeks later it's grown and you're reaping, or a day later it's grown and you're reaping. No! The time for sowing and the time for reaping are in two different seasons.

You have to be patient, you have to trust the process and you have to keep being persistent and consistent until the results show up. I can't stress that enough, I really can't stress that enough. If there's anything to take away from this entire course, there's so much value packed into this course, it's unbelievable.

And I'm going to want you to watch this over and over again. Just take it in over and over again. Go back after this and watch it over and over again. It's your manual, it's your Bible, it's your everything. Do not do anything else other than this if you want to grow your clothing brand from scratch to six figures. Use these paid traffic examples as Bible and do not veer away or steer away from them. Keep using them and doing them until the results show up for you.

There is massive value on how to build a clothing brand from scratch to six figures in this book. I look forward to hearing from you and hearing your stories on how this book transforms your startup clothing brand, I really do look forward to it.

Go away, digest it and I am really looking forward to hearing from you guys or you should I say, letting me know exactly what this book has done for you. If you've got any questions or concerns, feel free to hit us up on YouTube, on our Instagram, on our Twitter.

Head to our website www.webrandyou.co.uk, check out all of our products, all of our latest blog posts.

We're on a mission to help you guys grow, empower you guys with the tools you need to grow your clothing brand from scratch to six figures.

Wish you all the best

Lightning Source UK Ltd.
Milton Keynes UK
UKHW021833240123
415900UK00009B/508